COLLEGE CONTRACT

❧

Authentic Dialogue with
College Bound Children

❧

Written By John Honeycutt

ISBN: 1-4196-5552-3
ISBN-13: 9781419655524

Visit www.booksurge.com to order additional copies.

Contents

Prologue

In the US, our collective definition of an "adult" differs from beliefs of a hundred years ago. Recent decades have perhaps unintentionally encouraged legal adults to remain adolescent in many ways—remaining financially dependent on their parents even after receiving a four-year college degree. I'd like to contribute to reversing that trend.

My Love Letter

To: Danielle Honeycutt, Student

From: John Honeycutt, Dad

Re: Agreement for Understanding

Danielle, this note may seem overwhelming, unnecessary, and perhaps even initially offensive. I recognize this. Even so, it is out of love that I have drafted it. Our relationship changes on your upcoming birthday when you become legally an adult. Even if we wanted our relationship to remain the same, it would not. Partially because of the law of the land, partially because of cultural expectations, and partially because it is an appropriate time for our relationship to change – our relationship will change.

The change does not diminish my love for you. I am extremely proud of you and for you. This is an exciting time for a young adult to become free and independent. I'm glad that you have made it to this point and I will continue to pray for your safety, well-being, and your happiness. I want great things for you.

As you read through these paragraphs, please bear in mind that I am possibly, for the first time ever, treating you as an adult. This document is absolutely what I would do with any adult—family member or not—when making a decision, commitment, and agreement amounting to tens of thousands of dollars. Please do not take this effort lightly and please do not avoid genuinely contemplating through the muck and details.

Doing this together will decrease disagreement between you and me over the next few years. Also, it holds you and me accountable. You will have substantially more responsibility, and freedom to choose—with your responsibility, you must also be accountable. I hope this process serves to teach you full accountability so you can be and achieve the great things God has in store for you.

Going through this exercise, you and I will be much further ahead than most parents and their newly minted adult children. We will argue some points, come to resolution, and agree to move forward. In many ways I have cherished the drafting of this. But I also worry. Even though I have attempted to be fair and complete, I worry you will struggle with some aspects of this—possibly even fail in certain areas. Danielle, I have a difficult time watching either you or James encounter difficulties—especially failure. Still, I recognize I must allow you the risk of failure so you can relish the success on your own. It is right to put down on paper my thinking and provide you a road map.

Now bear in mind that the first time you read through this, the document is intended to be a DRAFT. I may have left out an important detail, I may have poorly estimated something, or I may be asking too much or too little of you. I expect and hope you will have ideas, hesitancy, and issues with some of these things. That is part of the process. On the other hand—this is also serious—I am not expecting a broad-sweeping set of counteroffers. Finalizing our contract needs to be collaborative, done in the spirit of mutual agreement—not in the spirit of concessions and compromise.

We will need to reach agreement—signed agreement—prior to my investing substantially in your education beyond high school. Unlike getting you through high school, where it has been my duty as your father and as your custodian, this is a different circumstance. I am not required to make this additional investment of my time, effort, and money to launch you into adulthood with an improved chance of being successful in a career, and possibly more successful in life. With this contract, I am offering to support you over the next four years with up to <<$amount>> through cash, payments, and other items.

You can choose to reject the offer entirely, but understand that I will not make such a sizeable investment without clarity of expectations, objectives, assumptions, and accountability. We will need to go through the effort of collaboratively adjusting this contract to our mutual satisfaction, or you will need to simply reject it entirely and be a fast adult on your own. I'm not being harsh, I am simply being honest.

As you read through this, please ask yourself a few questions when you come to a point where you are either bored to tears, or perhaps even greatly offended. Ask yourself this:

- What is my dad teaching me right now, in this sentence?

- Can I do this? Will I be able to honor my side of the commitment here?

- Is this fair? If it truly doesn't seem fair, then how can I support my opinion?

- If I request a change in this area, what other areas might need to be adjusted?

- At the completion of the agreement, will I be better off than if I don't do this?

- When something seems unreasonable, is it simply unreasonable for me, or would it be unreasonable for everyone?

Before getting into the details, I want to reemphasize that I love you and want great things for you, Danielle. I look forward to the day I am the father of the bride, the proud grandpa, and the old man visited by his little girl who happens to be in her thirties or forties. I want you to experience the college life, to get a four-year college degree, and to find a career (be it as an at-home mom, teacher, or salesperson) that energizes you and makes you content. This is the best I know how to do, and it the best I can reasonably afford. Please take care as you review the paragraphs and prepare your ideas and thoughts. Thank you.

– Love, Dad.

Athlete loaded with high credit card debt despite a full-ride scholarship.

Kai Ying has a full-tuition soccer scholarship to a well-known private university in Texas. The estimated annual value of her scholarship totals nearly $30,000 per year. Kai Ying completes her education successfully, but is deep in credit card debt on graduation.

She reluctantly accepts her parents' offer. Her childhood bedroom will serve as a rent-free apartment for one year, on the condition she uses her income to pay off debt. Kai Ying, now a twenty-two-year-old college graduate from an impressive university, turns her entire paycheck over to her mother for the next twelve months.

Her mother distributes a small allowance back to Kai Ying each week, funneling most of Kai Ying's paycheck to pay off her lavishly spent credit card debt. The situation is not pleasant for Kai Ying or her parents.

While in college, Kai Ying was ill informed about credit usage, credit card debt, and the realities of getting out of it once in it. Her parents had been unaware of the situation until now—but it is too late. They incorrectly assumed their daughter was smartly maximizing her hefty scholarship.

How can a young woman with $120,000 in scholarships end up with a pile of credit card debt?

Deserving son shocked at squandering parents.

Jacob has been a model high school student with the aptitude and desire to become an engineer. He lives with his parents and younger brothers and sisters in a beautiful, large home. His parents encourage Jacob's college aspirations and say they will support him.

It is now time to pay tuition at the local university. Jacob presents the cost to his parents. He is understandably surprised and deeply disappointed to learn their definition of "support" does not mean what he thought.

Until just now, he had no idea his parents lived so far beyond their income. Jacob can remain living at their home, remain on their car insurance plan, and eat their food. However, they do not intend to pay for his tuition, books, and other fees. Jacob recovers, but starts much more slowly than he had planned and aspired to.

Do you know any parents living beyond their means, with college-bound children on the horizon?

Waitress laments self-wavering.

Jill, an energetic waitress, expresses regret about not having more encouragement. Jill has been paying her own way through school, but is also carving her own path in understanding how the adult world really works.

Her parents loved and supported her while she was under their care. Five years ago, they sent her off on her own. She acknowledges that her parents were not in a position to support her financially, but she believes they could have invested time. Perhaps more coaching or counseling would have been helpful.

She deals with their lack of any financial support by working hard. But she has struggled in the absence of their emotional support. Several times she has vacillated between continuing with school or quitting altogether and making the best of her other options.

Now at twenty-three, Jill has two more years ahead of her to complete a degree. She is resolute today, but feels she could have done things faster with a little more guidance, and more emotional support from her parents.

Were Jill's parents right or wrong in their approach?

Musical scholarship discarded.

Navin is a musician. He accepts a scholarship to a prestigious college one state south of his home. His mother gladly commits supplemental financial support.

Navin pursues music for his first two years. Tuition and most other costs are underwritten by his scholarship money. His mother's support remains supplemental.

Without discussing his decision with his mother, he independently withdraws from his school to move back home. His mother is taken aback and finds herself in an awkward situation. She has verbally committed to helping her son complete college. But she has assumed he would make use of the music scholarship.

They work it out and find balance in the situation. Navin's mother increases her financial contributions to her son's education, along with extending him free room and board.

She loves her son deeply, and is glad he is continuing his education. Still, she regrets being unclear in her verbal commitments and not being consulted about Navin's decision.

Was it right for Navin to make his decision without consulting his mother?

Parents belatedly switch to tough love.

Diane has been coddled, spoiled, and overprotected throughout her life. Her father is in a lucrative position that easily affords an upper-middle-class lifestyle and ample allowances to his children.

Diane has not lived away from home before, and has never been out from under her parents' oversight. As a freshman she seemed to do reasonably well. As a sophomore she seemed to stall out a bit.

In the most recent two years, Diane has *gone off the deep end.*

Her freedom away from home has been unfettered and unchecked. While receiving daddy's money each month, Diane has been using the rent money for other purposes, and not attending class. At first her dad's deep pockets pay the late rent payments directly for a second time, while he believes his daughter's explanations and concocted stories.

Finally, her father unearths the uncomfortable truth. Diane has been making many poor decisions—and engaging in some illegal activity. Diane's parents remove her from school for recovery. Diane, at twenty-three, has failed to complete her degree, and has hit rock bottom.

Is tough love the right approach? Should tough-love happen earlier?

Upperclassmen break down crying during a freshman-level class.

Sheena and Maria, a junior and senior, break down in tears. If new freshmen with perfect credit scores are the "before," then they represent the "after" picture of college students caught in a credit card spiral. This is a freshman-level class that all students in their university are required to attend before graduating. Both deferred the class until now.

College students are inundated with easy access to high-interest credit cards offering quick fixes to temporary problems and a fast way to satisfy an impulsive desire to buy or do something.

This class teaches basics in budgeting, checkbook balancing, and fundamental credit concepts. These young women already know firsthand the woes of being in a credit whirlwind. They have mastered the art of using one card to pay off others, and then repeat the cycle the following month.

They actually do cry—out loud—partially because they regret not taking the course earlier. Possibly, the course would have helped them avert their current difficulties. But a deliberate conversation from their parents or other mentors might have been helpful too.

How can intelligent young adults be so easily lured into the use of credit for unnecessary purposes?

Time-Tested Principles Find Traction in Today's Culture

The stories above represent dozens of similar stories I hear each month. In my travels to cities across the United States, parents and their adult children of all demographics share their stories of success and misfortune.

The great news is that not all college stories have tragic chapters and many have barely a hiccup of surprise. But more often than not, I am finding many parents and their adult college-bound children do not fully share a vision for the college years. Avoidable expenditures, mountains of debt, delayed or stretched-out time lines, and just plain stupid decisions happen.

The issues go both ways. Loving parents get surprised by their princess going off the deep end while a well-deserving engineering student discovers his parents have been living above their means. The issues frequently involve money—absolutely. But the issues are equally about miscommunication.

The time-tested principles I believe to be valuable today are straightforward:

1. Stick to a realistic budget.

2. Communicate the full truth.

This book aims to improve how and when money is invested in young adults for their college education, and to improve dialogue between you, the parent, and your college-bound student. This book will have succeeded when you and your child save money on the college journey and when you begin a deeper, more authentic dialogue with your child.

College Contract™

Authentic Conversations with College-Bound Children

Definition One

College Contract™ (n): A signed, written agreement between a college-bound adult and another adult. The agreement describes unique understandings between the parties. A budget, expectations, limitations, and related circumstances are put in writing. The contract covers a specific time period.

Characteristics of a College Contract™:

- Describes budget, expectations, and limitations

- Is written and signed by both parties

- Is for a specified time frame

- Is tailored to each situation

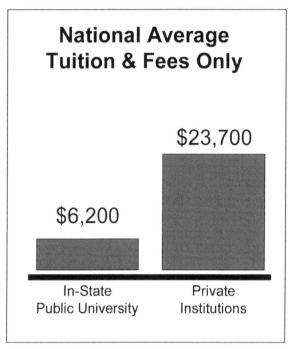

Source: College Board, Trends in
College Pricing 2007

Definition Two

College Contract™ (v): A process creating ongoing, authentic
dialogue between parents and their children in college.

Characteristics of a College Contract™:

• Speeds up independence

• Produces smarter decisions

- Improves communication

- Saves money

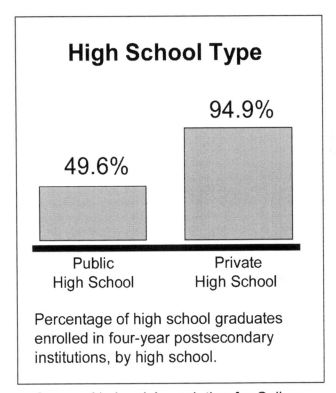

High School Type

49.6%

94.9%

Public
High School

Private
High School

Percentage of high school graduates
enrolled in four-year postsecondary
institutions, by high school.

Source: National Association for College
Admission Counseling's "State of College
Admission, 2005-06"

"By the time a man realizes that maybe his father was right, he usually has a son who thinks he's wrong." Charles Wadworth.

Who, me?

You can benefit from this book, regardless of the size of your child's college fund. While the College Contract™ tackles the subject of money, it more significantly produces authentic conversations. Generation Y savors authenticity. This is not the time to be fact-bending or vague. Who else but you to be genuine, accurate—and deal with your child as an adult?

What now?

Your child is either recently an adult or soon to be a legal adult. You have done reasonably well in raising him. You provided the basics: food, clothing, and shelter. You also gave safety, guidance, support, encouragement, discipline, friendship, health care, and other provisions. You may have provided much more than this, going far beyond mere basics. Are you to continue? Should you put her out on her own? What do you do now?

Starting When?

Even if unintentional, you started the dialogue years ago. The College Contract™ simply formalizes what you have already communicated in other ways. It stimulates authentic dialogue, setting in motion an adult-to-adult conversation. The contract is not an end unto itself. It reveals what you hope for your child, and allows your child to do the same with you. It takes time and effort to fully compose a College Contract™. Done well, the payoff will be lower costs, smarter decisions, and a faster education. Once drafted and signed, it should become an active reference document for both of you. The contract becomes central to an ongoing dialogue for the next few years. It takes time and effort, so why not get started now?

Where do I start?

The best starting place is from what you already know. You already have a sense for what you want to do and what you are able to do. Your child has a set of assumptions also. Complicating things a bit are the differences between you at age eighteen and your newly minted adult of today. Still, assumption gaps aside, the best place to start is by putting your thoughts in writing. This book will guide you through one way of doing it—but more importantly, your child deserves to receive *straight talk* from you before launching into college. Even in the best circumstances, it is unlikely your thinking is in lockstep with your adult child's assumptions. Where better to start than from what you already know?

Why this?

The College Contract™ assists you in clarifying your aspirations for your child. Clear boundaries and expectations are established. The College Contract™ enables you to think through what you can realistically *pony up* and what your child will need to independently bring to the table. The College Contract™ goes both ways. It puts limits, responsibility, and accountability on your child's shoulders and on your shoulders. The College Contract™ helps both of you say what you mean in a straightforward, authentic way. Even if you already talk straight with your child, why not avoid confusion and launch your new adult into college with clarity?

Is this really necessary?

No. For decades, parents and their children have gotten along just fine without a formal contract for college pursuits. Some of today's parents and their children do not need this process at all. A better question for most of us is whether it is valuable and worthwhile.

OK, so is this valuable and worthwhile?

Yes. The College Contract™ process is valuable in several ways. It will likely save money—for the simple fact that a budget is a key component of the College Contract™. Making a budget and sticking to it is a *no-brainer*, but few adults as a parent-child team actually do this together. If you fail to make a written budget and agree upon the budget, then you have not actually made a College Contract™. Equally as important, the College Contract™ process improves the way you and your adult child will communicate over the next few years. Other positive outcomes include better decision making and faster completion of the degree sought.

How much financial support should I provide?

Your initial reaction to this question might range from no support at all to underwriting an absolutely free ride. This book advocates something in between. This book will help you get to the right answer for you. Not all of us expect our children to attend college while others of us presume they will. This book is relevant to a spectrum of support. Bear in mind that while "support" is most frequently equated to finances, support comes in other flavors too. Take this journey together. Construct a College Contract™ tailored to your situation.

One of the biggest concerns for many families is how they are going to pay their children's college expenses. In academic year 2007–2008, the average cost for full-time undergraduates to attend four-year public institutions, including tuition, fees, room and board, stands at $14,600. The average for tuition, fees, room and board cost stands at well over $30,000 for private institutions. Note these figures do not include health-related expenses and insurance, transportation and automobile repair expense, or a range of other ancillary costs.

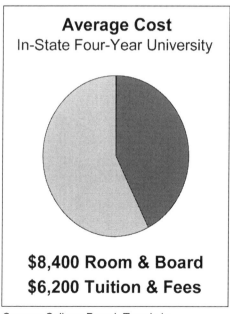

Average Cost
In-State Four-Year University

$8,400 Room & Board
$6,200 Tuition & Fees

Source: College Board, Trends in
College Pricing 2007

From the mid-1990s through 2007, inflation-adjusted tuition jumped 40 percent. Increases include public and private colleges and universities. During this same period, family incomes of those most likely to have college-age children rose only 8 percent. Projections beyond 2007 vary widely. But, even conservative estimates suggest continued increased costs.

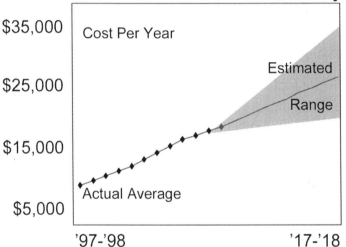

Average Total Cost
Public Four-Year University

Sources: College Board, Department of Labor, Compiled Projections.

Such price increases have made it difficult for families from most income levels to pay for college. College savings accounts, part-time jobs, scholarships, loans, grants, and family support can contribute toward the cost. Many institutions are beginning to slow the rate of increases.

Still, real attention is still warranted toward these facts. Beyond the undergraduate program, cost remains difficult for many to pay.

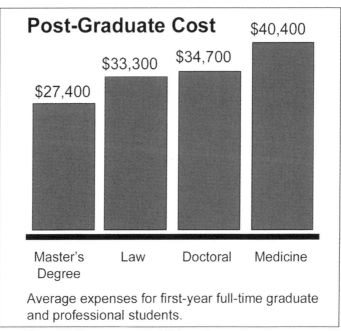

Post-Graduate Cost

$27,400 — Master's Degree
$33,300 — Law
$34,700 — Doctoral
$40,400 — Medicine

Average expenses for first-year full-time graduate and professional students.

Source: Department of Education

Will things change between me and my child?

In a word, yes. In the United States, there are millions of others like you and me. We span two generations, often called baby boomers and Generation X. Our group includes all economic conditions. Some of us have toiled through poverty. Some of us have had a different kind of struggle dealing with affluence. A great many of us, perhaps obviously, are in the middle. Whether in the middle or at either extreme, all of us have been working to get our children grown. We are either there already, or we are fast approaching that place—the place with adult children. Like it or not, our relationship changes when our children become legal adults. Now that we are done with the childhood and teenage phases, what changes will take place in the relationship with our children? What do these changes look like while in college?

Authenticity 101

"The father who does not teach his son his duties is equally guilty with the son who neglects them." Confucius BC 551-479, Chinese Ethical Teacher, Philosopher.

"Courage is what it takes to stand up and speak; courage is also what it takes to sit down and listen." Winston Churchill.

Truth is, you started the College Contract™ dialogue years ago—we all did. We mumble something under our breath, we react in a particular way, we make offhanded comments, we weave humor and sarcasm into our stories, and we participate in some activities while rejecting others. All of these things "say something."

Other examples of silent and perhaps intentional dialogue come in a variety of forms. It could be through the artwork or family photographs we hang on our walls, or even the jobs we appear to like or dislike, and it goes on and on. Most of what we communicate to others is not just through our spoken words. We say things to others in the way that we live, in the things we possess, in the way we react, in the tone of our voice, in gestures we use.

The diagram below illustrates a sampling of the variety of ways we communicate. All of these methods are valid, and even necessary. In this instance, I am advocating deliberate and active communication through the use of a written contract. You and your child will explicitly express your viewpoints to each other through the contracting process.

A contract is similar to other active communication methods to express viewpoints. Spoken communication can provide directives and advice. But, these rely on memory and recollection. A written checklist is helpful, but a contract provides much more detail. A contract reduces the risk of overlooking an important point. This makes for authentic dialogue.

Ways We Communicate		Concepts		Viewpoints	
		Precedence	Modeled	Spoken	Written
Active	Explicit	Position Statements	Demos and Tours	Directives	Contracts
	Suggested	Position Interests	Joint Research	Advice	Checklists
Passive	Implicit	Historical Choices	Body Language	Metaphor	Stories
	Contextual	Shared Experiences	Home Environment	Speaking in Code	Parables

Maybe your college-bound child has fully internalized everything you have been communicating the past eighteen years. Maybe your child does not need additional guidance, financial advice, or financial support. Chances are you have a lot to offer, even if not in financial support, then through what I call an authentic dialogue.

For starters, scan the list of discussion points below. Browse the list while considering your viewpoint and your child's viewpoint on each item. Some items will be straightforward for you, others may be more controversial. When your child was a minor, these subjects were clear cut. Your opinion was the right opinion. With your adult-child these subjects become blurred. You may assume your child shares your viewpoint. But now, who is responsible for making decisions around these subjects? Who is now accountable for outcomes related to these topics?

- Abortion expenses

- Bank overdrafts and overage charges

- Beauty services such as facials, manicures, pedicures, waxing, and massage

- Bodybuilding supplements

- Cable television subscriptions

- Cigarettes, liquor

- Cosmetic dentistry, such as tooth whitening

- Cosmetic surgery

- Credit card origination fees and interest expenses

- Damages, fines, or other fees related to the operation of a vehicle

- Devices, including mobile phones and personal digital assistants (PDAs)

- Diet pills/drinks

- Drug paraphernalia

- Energy supplements

- Formal wear for special events, including dances, showers, and school celebrations

- Fun money

- Furniture

- Gambling debt

- Gasoline

- Guns, including hunting rifles and handguns

- Health and fitness club memberships

- Hobby expenses such as a scrapbook, art collection, music collection

- Insurance (health and automobile)

- International studies related to a degree requiring travel abroad

- Investments

- Laptop or desktop technology

- Legal fees related to criminal or civil charges

- Linen, including towels and sheets

- Men's magazine subscriptions

- Mobile phone contracts

- Neon signs with beer advertisements

- Parking tickets, speeding tickets, or other citations

- Pet purchases, pet supplies, pet medical bills, other pet-related expenses

- Pots, pans, other kitchen items

- Promissory notes or other financial commitments

- Religious affiliation and worship

- Repairs of any type

- Season tickets to sporting events

- Tanning memberships

- Tattoos, body piercing, or removal costs for such items

- Taxes: federal, state, and local

- Travel expenses, including fuel and vacation expenses

- Voting and party affiliation

- Wedding expenses

- Weight loss techniques

You have probably discussed many important topics with your child about college. Helping a graduating high school student choose a college is a huge big deal. Introducing your child to some basics around the cost of college is also commendable. But think about this with me for a minute. Does your child truly have a grasp of the difference between $12,000 a year and $36,000 a year? Other than the second number being three times as big as the first number, most graduating high school seniors do not have a realistic way to internalize the magnitude of these costs, except that both numbers seem pretty big.

Beyond this, what happens when your first-year college student self-indulges with a six-month tanning membership, but then overdrafts the bank five times in one month? Most of us can count on getting a phone call asking for a bailout. Many of us will say no—but come on—these discussions are most typically held after the fact. I am advocating you get ahead of the issue and address it before it happens. Be explicit. Put your wisdom down in writing. Use your College Contract™ as a teaching device, and then rely on your College Contract™ to be the *bad guy* when the bank overdraft charges do occur.

The College Contract™ will help you shave down the big costs by establishing a realistic budget. But, among the most valuable benefits are the little things. Dialogue about benign subjects such as furniture, kitchen items, or even linen may surprise you. Ratchet things up a notch and discuss mobile phone contracts, gasoline, and fun money. Take things to a truly adult level and talk through subjects including guns, mixed-gender sleeping arrangements, gambling, abortion, investments, taxes, and gambling debt.

You and your child will not agree on everything—but that is exactly the point! The College Contract™ process helps you think through, discuss, and put down in writing the things you can agree on.

Sure, it is easier to defer tough subjects and passively hope everything will just work out on its own. I hope you rethink this approach. I strongly hope you instead actively communicate with your child in a new way. This is a vital time in his or her life.

Eventually, when a tough subject needs to be confronted, most people do work it out. The College Contract™ will not eliminate all tough situations. But you can lessen the issues that might have otherwise occurred out of naivety, ignorance, or misunderstanding.

How easy will this be for you? The answer for everyone is it takes some time and effort. But some of you will be more comfortable with the process than others.

I have put together a set of true/false statements to help you estimate how easy or how difficult this process might be for you and your child. This quiz is not scientific or validated with hundreds of people, but it will give you a reasonable idea of where you might land. I encourage you to read each true/false statement and tally the score. Avoid the temptation of giving yourself half a point for some statements. Let the statement be either true or false, not partially true or partially false. You will land in one of four broad groups described after the quiz.

About you

For each true statement, add one point (there are ten possible points).

(T/F) I have openly revealed my childhood and early adult years to my child

(T/F) I enforce consequences for my child's poor decisions

(T/F) I am good at sticking to a binding contract once it is agreed upon

(T/F) I teach my values through stories, metaphors, and by walking the talk

(T/F) I rarely, if ever, use money to solve a conflict

(T/F) The home I've provided to my child conveys my value system

(T/F) I frequently use checklists to manage my life and my child's life

(T/F) I make a budget and stick to it for my personal finances

(T/F) I speak simply and am easy to understand

(T/F) My home has little drama and little conflict

About your child

For each true statement, add one point (there are ten possible points).

(T/F) My child has successfully held at least one job for more than six months

(T/F) My child has proactively researched one or more colleges without my help

(T/F) My child expects to significantly help pay for college through work or scholarships

(T/F) My child accepts responsibility for poor decisions without blaming others

(T/F) My child follows the rules and appreciates guidelines

(T/F) My child has not been overindulged

(T/F) My child rarely gets angry

(T/F) My child communicates with me exceptionally well

(T/F) My child understands and accepts consequences for poor decision making

(T/F) My child solves difficult interpersonal situations with little or no assistance from others

Scoring/Indicators

Add all points together and find the category where you land (there are twenty total possible points).

16–20 points—You and your child already interact with the world consistent with the College Contract™ process. You may be tempted to skip over key sections in the book because much of it will seem like common sense to you. However, don't skip sections. Go through the entire process. You will clarify some otherwise fuzzy subjects. Again—don't yield to the temptation to skip over sections.

10–15 points—You and your child interact with the world in several areas consistent with the College Contract™ process. You will find some things to be common sense and will be uncomfortable confronting other concepts. Don't do the easy stuff while skipping over the harder stuff. It's the harder part that will probably bring you the most value.

5–9 points—You and your child are going to experience a new adventure together going through the College Contract™ process. The good news is that you are likely to be the biggest beneficiary of this book, assuming you are able to fully go through with it. The bad news is the process may seem unwieldy and difficult to you. You may be tempted to quit. Don't! Go talk to other adults with grown children. Listen to their stories and then come back to the book. It is you, possibly more than anyone else, I have written this book for.

0–4 points—You and your child are almost certainly going to find the College Contract™ process difficult. Please continue reading though. Chew on some of the concepts here. But, before taking things too far, work toward flipping a few more of the indicators on the quiz to true. Possibly, the biggest value this book has to offer you is in illustrating a different approach to some aspects of your life. Please note that I am not saying all of the statements represent the best way to live, although my personal belief is the statements tend to be a valid way of living. If you have landed in this category, challenge yourself to think through whether a few more of these statements could and should become true statements for you. Then, figure out how to make them flip true.

More about your score

The quiz is not intended to make a value judgment about you and your child. Rather, the quiz is entirely meant to help you predict how comfortable or difficult the College Contract™ process is likely to be to you. Low scores on the quiz indicate you may find the process more difficult than parent-child pairs with high scores. I recognize our culture thinks of low scores being bad and high scores being good. My personal belief is the statements tend to reflect good ways of living—but I recognize they are not the only way to live.

Summary

The College Contract™ formalizes what you *think* you have already communicated. It stimulates authentic dialogue. It sets in motion an adult-to-adult conversation. Most of us discuss the big picture and the basics with our college-bound students. We participate in a school tour, we talk about tuition rates, and we help our students apply for grants and scholarships. But these things skip over some of the richest discussion. The College Contract™ emphasizes a variety of important topics. Go on the school tour. Have the high-level money talk. But dig deeper too.

Many don't discuss difficult topics before sending their student off to school. Maybe, we avoid the topics. We may not say it aloud, but in our hearts we feel we remain entitled to a lot of decision making—especially if we provide significant financial support during the college years. In contrast, our children feel entitled to financial and emotional support while also feeling entitled to independence as a legal adult.

In a perfect world, this would be OK and circumstances would work out. Perfect world or not, most things do eventually get worked out. But we can do a better job in tackling difficult subjects head-on, sparing ourselves and our children from some strife at a later time.

The College Contract™ process is about having authentic dialogue with your child. The dialogue includes easy subjects such as towels, linens, and kitchen supplies. (Don't laugh—even these discussions can evoke emotion.) The process also encourages discussion around substantive topics. Some topics may elevate visceral disagreement. The process will not resolve all disagreements, but it does help.

Because we started the College Contract™ dialogue years ago with our children through direct and indirect ways, the process will not be equally easy for everyone. The quiz in this section helps you pinpoint how comfortable you might feel with the process. Regardless, my advice to all is:

- Avoid skipping sections

- Avoid doing only the easy parts

- Finish the process, don't give up

- Consider flipping a few more statements to true

"Getting your house in order and reducing the confusion gives you more control over your life. Personal organization some how releases or frees you to operate more effectively." Larry King, American TV Personality.

OK. It is now time to get down to business. It is time for getting your house in order. It is time for personal organization. This section outlines your upcoming semester in creating your College Contract™ with your child. It is time for authentic dialogue!

When I say "semester," I am not simply being cute in using school-like language. I literally mean a semester. This process will take you about three months to complete, beginning to end. You may be able to accelerate the time line, but three months is an appropriate amount of time to collaboratively draft and then sign your contract.

You need to be the judge of how detailed your contract should be. My prediction is that once you get started, you will discover several areas deserving additional attention. A reasonable length of a College Contract™ ranges from ten to thirty standard typewritten pages.

You will need to use a modern word processor. Most of us have computers at home or access to technology at our work. If by chance you do not have access to a computer and word processing software, make a visit to your local library and get assistance there. This book presumes the contracting process will be iterative. You and your child will necessarily need to collaborate on many points, make concessions on some important points, and make minor corrections here and there.

One more item is appropriate to mention. The examples used in the sections below are only slightly modified from actual paragraphs I used in the contract with my daughter. I was a single father for a number of years, and was my daughter's primary custodian. Before her high school graduation, I remarried. As such, my contract with my daughter is written from this perspective. In all cases, the examples can be adjusted to fit your circumstances. If you are married, divorced, the grandparent, an aunt/uncle, or have otherwise been a guardian or custodian, adjust the examples to fit your situation.

To get started, create a blank document with the following major headings, leaving the content blank for now:

Major Sections

College Contract

1. Love Letter
2. Overview
3. Primary Intentions
4. General Assumptions
5. Timing
6. Obligations & Commitments
7. Out of Scope
8. Personal Property
9. Family Residence
10. Financial Table
11. Special Circumstances
12. Signatures

Month 1 –

During the first month, you will get the process started and several of the key sections drafted. While the contract deals with financial prudence, as well as authenticity, this first month focuses more significantly on the big picture. Don't expect to identify all the details yet. Your contract should be clearly labeled as "DRAFT" at this point, with the mutual understanding that many of the details will be identified in future weeks.

You absolutely need to inform your child you intend to write a College Contract™ and you expect to sign the contract together before further investing your time, effort, and money in their college journey. Your child may not fully grasp what this means to them, yet. Even so, the earlier you start the dialogue, the better.

Using the document you created with the major section headings in place, begin to fill out some of the content as illustrated in the diagram labeled "Month"

This book includes sample content for each section. You may use the examples exactly as presented in this book— but more likely, you will need to use the examples as a guideline only. Your content should reflect your values, your expectations, and your capability to hold up your end of the agreement.

Of all the sections suggested, the "Love Letter" is the most personal, and deserves special attention. The other sections will be updated and modified over the next several weeks while you and your child discuss and learn from each other.

In contrast, the Love Letter will remain largely unchanged after initially sharing it with your child. As such, it deserves to be written in final form, rather than as a draft. For those parents who recognize they might have difficulty in "letting go" of their emerging adult children, the Love Letter serves the additional purpose of helping you let go.

You may be tempted to hurry through the other sections during the first month. I strongly suggest you avoid rushing the process. During the first month, you will begin to confirm and communicate your general ability to support your child financially. You will also begin listing "out-of-scope" items that could require quite a bit of discussion.

Actions to take during the first month:

- Discuss the idea

- Draft your Love Letter

- Draft your Primary Intentions

- Draft the General Assumptions

- Draft the Timing

- Draft the Obligations and Commitments

- Draft the Out of Scope List

- Share the initial draft with your child

- Discuss each section and take notes

Month 1

College Contract

1. **Love Letter**
2. Overview
3. **Primary Intentions**
4. **General Assumptions**
5. **Timing**
6. **Obligations & Commitments**
7. **Out of Scope**
8. Personal Property
9. Family Residence
10. Financial Table
11. Special Circumstances
12. Signatures

Month 2 –

During the second month, you will be diving into the details. Your contract should still be clearly labeled as "DRAFT," but it will start looking like a complete and final document. You are well on your way with authentic dialogue.

By now, your child should be keenly aware of the College Contract™. Your child should know what his or her role needs to be in finalizing the agreement. During the second month, your child should independently research costs of each line item listed in the Financial Table.

Emerging adults in the United States have widely varied understandings of the "cost of things." Some teenagers pay their own automobile insurance, and others are sheltered from those costs. Health care, utility, and mobile phone bills are other examples of expenses your adult child needs to understand. These important topics, along with the costs of tuition, books, fees, and food deserve specific attention.

Most families do not have enough savings to fund a four-year college education. But even for those families with enough saved, there remains a range of financial topics deserving discussion.

The media regularly reports the debt spiral that many young adults encounter during their college years to fill the gap. Most books and college resources focus on where to get loans, grants, and other sources of payment. You definitely need to explore these options but the College Contract™ approaches the issue from a different angle--a budget.

Let's face it—making a budget is boring. If your child has been isolated from financial decision making, this exercise may be difficult for him or her. But as your child becomes independent, it is appropriate to transfer responsibility and accountability for financial obligations.

Make a backup copy of the document you created in the first month, then, fill out the content for sections suggested in the diagram labeled "Month 2." This book includes sample content for each of the sections. For the sections suggested for month two, you will need to use the examples as a guideline only. Your content will need to specifically reflect your family's situation.

The Financial Table serves as the centerpiece to the College Contract™. The table identifies financial support you will be providing to your child. Your child needs to understand that the difference between the actual cost and your financial support will need to come from somewhere else. A less expensive school may be required. A scholarship or grant may be required. Work or work programs may be necessary. Extending the time from four years to six may be appropriate. Or loans might be required.

Actions to take during the second month:

• Update earlier sections, if necessary

• Draft the Personal Property section

• Draft the Family Residence section

• Draft the Financial Table

• Draft the Special Circumstances section

• Share the updated document

• Discuss each section and take notes

Month 2

College Contract

1. Love Letter
2. Overview
3. Primary Intentions
4. General Assumptions
5. Timing
6. Obligations & Commitments
7. Out of Scope
8. **Personal Property**
9. **Family Residence**
10. **Financial Table**
11. **Special Circumstances**
12. Signatures

Month 3 –

You will finalize each of the earlier sections and complete the Overview and Signature sections during the third month.

The Overview Section is saved for last. It summarizes the other sections. Think of the Overview as an executive summary or as the one-page synopsis of the most important pieces of your College Contract™.

The Signature section contains legal jargon and provides a place to sign your College Contract™ and have it notarized.

If your child is a legal adult by this time, print the final copies and sign them in front of a notary public, to make the contract official.

Your child should be actively engaged in finalizing the detail of each section—making suggestions, raising issues and concerns, and coming to agreement with you. Certain ideas for incentives and penalties might emerge during this final month. For example, you may be inclined to pay a premium for A's, but lesser amounts for B's and C's. Another approach might be to fund tuition for any passing scores, but not for failed grades. Similar incentives might be appropriate for certain cost savings. For example, you might consider awarding a 20 percent cash bonus for any scholarships received and used, up to a certain amount.

Specific issues unique to your family situation and value system deserve explicit agreement. If you and your child are unable to agree on a particular point, consider documenting both points of view. Recognize that resolution might not be possible for some issues. An agreement to disagree might be the best you can achieve.

You will also want to include enough "wiggle room" in the contract to accommodate unforeseen circumstances in the future. A few examples of this include:

- Job layoff

- Incapacitation

- Illnesses or accidents

- Acts of God and nature

- Wartime requirements

- Decisions to marry or have children

- Other life events

Because a written contract implies a certain degree of legal responsibility for both parties, it is prudent to include a few standard clauses in your contract. Examples of these suggested clauses are provided in the "Include Signatures" chapter of this book.

Make a backup copy of the document you created in the second month, and then complete the remainder of the document, making all final edits and corrections.

Actions to take during the third month:

- Finalize all earlier sections

- Summarize the entire document in the Overview Section

- Include all appropriate "legalese" paragraphs in the Signature Section

- Print two copies for you and your child to make a final review.

- Make any final corrections and changes.

- Print final copies and sign in front of a notary public

- Consider filing one notarized copy of the Agreement with a court

Month 3

College Contract

1. Love Letter
2. **Overview**
3. Primary Intentions
4. General Assumptions
5. Timing
6. Obligations & Commitments
7. Out of Scope
8. Personal Property
9. Family Residence
10. Financial Table
11. Special Circumstances
12. **Signatures**

Write Your Love Letter

"For every one of us that succeeds, it's because there's somebody there to show you the way out." Oprah Winfrey, American TV Personality, Producer, Actor, Author.

Your Love Letter to your child should be drafted first, and placed as the first section in your College Contract™. This launches your authentic dialogue.

Here, you have an opportunity to concretely express your feelings toward your soon-to-be-an-adult child, and simultaneously offer your own wisdom.

Use the Love Letter (at the beginning of the book) that I wrote to my daughter as an example, but take enough time to tailor your letter to suit your specific situation and your child.

My letter is about two pages long when printed on standard 8½ × 11-inch paper. But, the specific length of your letter is less relevant than the intention of the letter. The letter will ideally reflect some things entirely unique to the two of you.

Include a reference to the nature of coming changes in your relationship. While many things will remain the same, some things truly will change—like it or not. If you are likely to offer significant financial support to your child, mention it here. It is absolutely appropriate to explicitly state that your financial support is optional, and not required (unless, of course, for some reason it actually is required).

Avoid going overboard on defending your intention to have a signed contract. But, it is appropriate to highlight that you would not enter into any financial obligation without a clearly written, agreed-upon contract.

Would you buy or sell a house without a contract? You would probably not do this.

Would you buy or sell a car without a contract? Even the purchase of a car typically includes some type of written contract.

Adults enter into contracts on a regular basis for their larger decisions and purchases. We have employment contracts, transactional contracts for appliances, and even colleges and universities require written and signed applications and agreements.

Your minor child may not have been aware how prevalent the idea of a contract is—perhaps it is so interwoven with our culture, that you have not thought much about it either. Here, in your Love Letter, bring out the fact that you are treating your child as an adult through this process.

I suggest drafting your Love Letter in Week 1 because it will set the tone for the remainder of the contract. Of all the sections, it is both the easiest and most difficult to write. It is easy, because it can come from the heart, and requires less analysis and thinking. It is also difficult because it will begin establishing a new boundary and context between you and your child. The letter writing may even be emotional for you, especially if this is your first child to become an adult.

You may want to wait a week or so before showing it to your child. Allow yourself some time to think through things, and begin putting some of the more difficult things on paper.

Write Your Overview

The Overview should be the second section in your College Contract™, but you'll want to write it last.

Do not spend time on the Overview until after you have made significant progress in the other sections. Simply include a heading called "Overview" in your document until about Week 9.

Use the overview to summarize the main points of each section. But the overview should also serve as a "legal-sounding" portion of the document.

A few key concepts are important to emphasize in your overview:

- Summarize the purpose of the agreement (Section 3).

- Summarize your expectations (Section 4).

- Summarize the time frame covered by the agreement (Section 5).

- Clarify that the agreement is made without duress.

- Explicitly state the agreement has been adjusted to reflect the ideas and intentions of both you and your child.

- Provide a clause for omissions not invalidating the agreement.

- Provide for the possibility that the agreement might require refinement at some future time.

- Include reference to your home county, or other legal jurisdiction, to underscore how the agreement would be evaluated, if ever needed.

- Clarify that the agreement is not intended to replace normal, day-to-day interaction.

An example of my Overview is provided below. Bear in mind that your Overview should reflect your specific situations.

It is unlikely that a College Contract™ would become the basis for a litigious situation between the parent and child. However, I suppose it would be possible—and if many thousands of people decide to follow this suggestion, I imagine some unfortunate situations might in fact turn litigious. I hope not. But—for clarity—you might ask a licensed attorney to review this section in particular. That is your call.

More than likely, however, something similar to the example Overview here will suffice for most situations.

Note the examples in this book presume an agreement between the adult-child and one parent. State laws vary, so that an agreement with only one parent may legally bind the spouse.

EXAMPLE

This College Contract™ (Agreement) serves multiple purposes. The primary purpose centers on the relationship between Danielle and John. The agreement covers the period beginning (beginning date) through (ending date). This agreement outlines the daughter-and-father relationship from a financial perspective for the daughter's education. This agreement describes the father's expectations associated with the daughter's pursuit of higher education.

This Agreement is made willingly and without duress between the father and daughter. This Agreement has been reviewed by both parties. It reflects both parties' interests, concerns, assumptions, and obligations. This Agreement outlines a framework for the relationship, but omissions or oversights may exist. Any omission or oversight does not invalidate the agreement. Some aspects may require modification or adjustment during the agreement period. If portions of the agreement require modification to comply with laws, or have been agreed upon by both parties, then that portion may be adjusted without invalidating remaining portions of the agreement. For the purposes of enforcement, this agreement falls under the jurisdiction of (county name and state).

Both parties agree that while the Agreement is binding, both parties can and will interact and communicate with each other. This agreement is not intended to replace or serve as a substitute for normal interactions, dialogue, and other typical family-related actions. The agreement is not intended to restrict normal day-to-day activities; rather it is intended to be supplemental to clarify mutual understanding up front, rather than after the fact in unforeseeable circumstances, as well as with likely events.

Write Your Primary Intentions

This section represents what most parents and their college-bound children already *verbally* do with each other. Writing down your intentions, and writing down what you believe to be the intentions of your child might yield some surprising findings.

To some extent, this section might be labeled with the cliché "Motherhood, and Apple Pie." In a way, this section describes high-level concepts that are relatively easy to agree on. This section establishes alignment between you and your child, without getting down into the bug dust. It is a great way to practice your authentic dialogue.

Primary intentions and guiding principles are outlined in this section. The intentions of both you and your child should be listed. Also the guiding principles provide a generalized outline of how the agreement will work over the course of time.

Two examples are provided below. Because the phrases "Primary Intention" and "Guiding Principles" may seem odd to some people, I've listed some alternative ways to express these concepts. You may want to choose one of these alternatives as the title for your section on Primary Intentions.

Primary Intentions are the same thing as:

- Main Purpose

- Shared Goals

- Expectations

Guiding Principles are the same as:

- Code of Conduct

- Standards of Interaction

- Shared Beliefs

EXAMPLE 1 – recommended

Overview

This section summarizes the primary intentions of each party. Both parties recognize that life circumstances can alter intentions of an individual or a group. But these intentions provide the underpinning to our Agreement. They provide justification for having this Agreement in place.

Student's Intentions

- Student intends to pursue a four-year college education. The program will be for a bachelor of arts (BA) or bachelor of science (BS) degree at an accredited university.

- Student intends to enroll, remain enrolled, and complete the degree-bound program beginning January 2007. The completion date will be no later than December 2010.

Parent's Intentions

- Parent intends to support Student financially, within limits, in her pursuit of a higher-education, degree-bound program.

- Parent intends to support Student during this period through fatherly advice and guidance. Various material goods may be required from time to time. He also offers continued love and affection.

Guiding Principles

- Both parties will communicate openly and frequently about circumstances, financial and otherwise, that may have an impact on this agreement.

- This agreement can be annulled by mutual consent by a written "Cancellation of Agreement" document, if signed and fully agreed to by both parties.

- Verbal commitments that do not materially alter the spirit or intention of the agreement can be made at any time. For the purpose of defining "material," this means a verbal commitment related to finances of $10 or less in any given month.

- Any changes to this agreement that are material, financial, or otherwise, must be agreed to in writing by both parties.

- "Special Circumstances" are described in a later section. In the event a special circumstance occurs, this agreement may become null and void. Or, a six-month gap and six-month extension as specified in each special circumstance identified may be necessary.

EXAMPLE 2 – a simpler alternative.

Expectations of Student

- Ask for help when it is needed

- Attend classes

- Avoid breaking the law

- Communicate important things to the parent

- Follow rules set by the college

- Graduate within four years of starting

- Keep a respectable grade point average

- Remain organized

- Strive to perform well

- Use private study time wisely

- Work part-time when you are able

Expectations of Parent

- Facilitate access to transportation

- Listen and provide advice when asked.

- Pay for selected portions of college costs

Write Your General Assumptions

This section may initially seem easy. For many, this section will be somewhat difficult. Assumptions are similar to your beliefs. Another way to think of assumptions is to write down your "best guess" or "theory" about how the next four years will play out. Assumptions serve as the "hypothesis" for the next few years. Getting these paragraphs right is absolutely a form of authentic dialogue.

Your assumptions section should focus primarily on financially oriented aspects of the contract. If an assumption proves false, then the subsequent components of the contract may not remain valid.

Categories to cover include

4. Assumptions

Financial Aid
Extraneous Expenses
Emergency Expenses
Requests for Money
Shared Savings Incentive
Proof of Expenses
Funding from Other Sources
Accumulation of Debt
Taxes and Tax Status

EXAMPLE

Financial Aid.

Student will make full and reasonable attempts, on a continuous basis, to secure financial aid, especially in the form of scholarships, grants, or other nonrepayable forms of aid. Each semester, Student will provide evidence to Parent, in the form of photocopies, that she has actively applied for one or more forms of scholarships totaling no less than $1,000 each semester from any variety or combination of sources. Parent acknowledges that Student may be unsuccessful in securing any scholarships or grants. This assumption is that Student will make a true effort to secure scholarships, not that she will in fact obtain scholarships.

Unnecessary Expenses.

Student will avoid unnecessary expenses, generally defined as those above and beyond that needed to live modestly, during the agreement period.

Avoid Additional Requests.

Except as outlined in this agreement, Student will avoid requesting additional funds, cash, or similar financial instruments, including prepaid credit cards, for example, from others during the agreement period—especially from Parent.

Emergency Expenses.

Medical necessity and transportation necessity are excluded from the definition of "additional requests." In the case of emergency situations, Parent and Student mutually agree and understand that Student, as an adult, is responsible for her own emergency expenses, but Parent, as Student's father may desire to assist even though he is under no obligation to do so.

Shared Savings.

Solely upon Parent's discretion and Student's ability to live within the budget, Student may receive a reward. For example, if in the extreme, Student were able to secure a 100 percent scholarship, Parent might give Student 50 percent of the cost of her tuition in a lump sum cash payment at the completion of her degree program.

Major Declaration.

Upon selection and enrollment of a four-year university, Student will declare a major area of study within the first thirty semester credit hours. Student will make every effort to complete the majority of all course work required for the degree at the selected institution. The exception to this may be that for summer semesters, Student may elect to take course work at an alternate, local campus. Student may change her major declaration through the first sixty hours of completed course work.

Full-Time Student.

Student will take at least twelve credit hours per semester, with no fewer than thirty total credit hours taken and earned per year. While twelve credit hours will define the minimum, Student acknowledges she should maintain fifteen credit hours during fall and spring semesters. The summer term should provide a "cushion" for additional credit hours, should they be necessary to complete a four-year degree within four years or less.

Receipts.

Student will provide clear evidence to Parent, in the form of original receipts, and copies of original transcripts and grades, throughout the agreement period. Student will provide copies of all such receipts and transcripts packaged in a single envelope covering each month, and delivered to Parent no later than the fifteenth day of each month following the month expenses were incurred. These will serve to provide an audit trail for IRS statements and other purposes that may be required from time to time.

Separate Support.

Student and Parent jointly assume the Student's mother will provide supplementary support equaling < <amount> > per year. Student must keep a log of income received and communication (verbal, written, and otherwise) related to this separate support received from her mother.

Other Debt.

Student will refrain from indebting herself to credit cards, bank loans, student loans, personal loans, and similar debt without first seeking counsel and advice from Parent. The Parent advises Student to secure one credit card with a $300–$500 limit. This credit card would be used in limited circumstances. The Student should fully pay off the balance each month. The rational for having one credit card is twofold: to have available in case of emergency, and to begin building an exceptional credit history prior to graduation.

Tax Status.

Unless Parent communicates otherwise, Student will remain listed as a dependent for Internal Revenue Services purposes. If allowed by the IRS, this status will remain throughout the agreement period. This status would change if the Student marries during this period. Student will promptly pay any and all federal and/or state income tax related to income she may generate. She will promptly inform Parent of all income received, all taxes paid, and other related events.

Identify the Timing

This book has been written assuming the pursuit of a four-year degree within four years. Some situations might benefit from stretching out or compressing the time frame covered by the contract. For example, some may need to use a six-year time frame to spread out the expenses and allow the student to work a full-time job while enrolled only part-time. Talking through the pros and cons of different time frames has tremendous value. Remember to be authentic. Communicate real expectations.

Explicitly state the beginning and ending of the contractual period. Provide for variations in the timing due to unforeseen circumstances. Be clear about the start and stop of the contract.

Consider including a list of expenses incurred before you execute the contract. Specifically, list out college-related expenses incurred prior to the effective date of the contract. It is appropriate for your child to recognize you invested in their college *before* they even attended the first class.

- Preparatory classes

- Travel costs to tour colleges and universities

- Interview clothing

- Time spent filling out forms and applications

- Opportunity cost of other pursuits due to saving for college in advance

The reason for listing prior costs is twofold. First, to highlight your time, effort, and money invested in your child before having reached this point. But also, because the formal contract should begin after your child becomes a legal adult, it is appropriate to separate these *sunk* costs from future costs you are agreeing to assume.

EXAMPLE

This agreement begins December 1, 2006, and ends at midnight December 31, 2010, except that college preparation expenses may be counted and included as part of Parent's investment and financial support provided toward Student as outlined below:

- Automobile expenses including purchase, lease, repair, licensing, and fuel for the month of December 2006. ($Estimated Amount)

- SAT preparation classes and SAT test registration. ($Estimated Amount)

- Expenses for travel or research related to the selection of a school. ($Estimated Amount)

In the event of unforeseen occurrences, including war, natural catastrophe, or other acts of God, Parent may, at his sole discretion, extend the timing of this agreement at twelve-month increments, if in writing and agreed to by both parties.

Define the Obligations & Commitments

You and your child will deeply benefit from the authentic dialogue in this section. Obligations are similar to one's duty or responsibility. Obligations are kind of like a requirement. Commitments are related to obligations, but are more like vows or pledges. Another way of thinking about commitments is to equate them to promises.

The heading of Obligations and Commitments might alternatively be called Requirements and Promises.

6. Commitments

Per Year and Overall Maximum

Tuition, Books, Room, Food

Car, Fuel, Car Repair

Health Insurance & Co-Pay

Personal Care & Miscellaneous

EXAMPLE

Per Year Maximum—Except for the initial year, which may require a greater cost due to "start-up," in no instance will the financial support provided by Parent to Student exceed $18,000 in a one-year period. Parent will reserve judgment on this limitation in the case of an emergency situation for a medical and/or transportation crisis.

Overall Maximum—In no instance will the financial support provided by Parent to Student exceed $64,000 total during the agreement period. This amount includes all amounts itemized in the Financial Table as well as any loans from Parent to Student during the agreement period.

Reductions from Maximum—Parent and Student agree the maximum financial support will not exceed $18,000 per year. The total support will not exceed $64,000. Reductions from the maximum amounts will be reduced first by the student's mother's contributions. Other reductions from the maximum support will come from Student's selection of a modestly priced institution, and by scholarships and grants secured by Student. The Student will additionally contribute through some of the wages she earns during the period.

Tuition—This is money paid directly to the university or learning institution, typically on a "per hour enrolled" schedule. Tuition paid requires a receipt, and Student agrees to provide clear evidence to Parent of any and all tuition paid. Tuition costs may be deductible for federal income tax purposes, and if so, Parent would necessarily elect to claim the deduction if allowed by law.

Room—This is money paid directly to the university or learning institution, or directly to a landlord or apartment operations organization. Room expenses, including utility expenses such as gas/water/electric, require a receipt to be provided to Parent. Student agrees to maintain a record of all such payments, and provide receipts for these expenses promptly upon Parent's request. If during the agreement period Student chooses to live at Parent's residence, the effective monthly room rate will be $125 per month.

Car—This represents the value of an automobile, truck, or similar transportation to be provided (and titled) in Student's name. This will be paid by the Parent. This is a one-time expense. All future car purchases by Student will not be paid for by Parent.

Food—This represents all food and related costs necessary for basic nutrition. This budgeted amount does not provide for entertainment or luxury dining in any way. Any food expenses above this budgeted amount are the sole responsibility of Student.

Health Insurance—If the Parent's health insurance provider permits Student to be covered during the agreement period, Student may continue to use the plan. The value listed here is about the cost of obtaining individual health insurance for a healthy, young adult. If Student chooses to select her own plan, but the family plan would allow her to continue, then no money will be set aside for health insurance coverage for Student.

If the family health insurance plan does not permit Student to be covered because of her age or residency, then Parent will provide the amount listed in the Financial Table for Student to purchase health insurance coverage on her own. Student must provide clear evidence of the cost of such insurance.

Car Repair—This provides for maintenance including oil changes, annual tune-ups, and for some modest, unexpected more expensive car repairs. Any repair or maintenance above this budgeted amount will require Student to pay it. Receipts for these expenses will be provided from Student to Parent upon request.

Loan—This represents the maximum "additional money" available to the Student from Parent. Loans will require Student's signature and acknowledgement that the money will be repaid. Repayment will be within twenty-four months from her graduation date or the termination of this agreement, whichever comes first. The loan will be noninterest bearing during the loan repayment time. Monthly payments will be computed by dividing the amount owed by twenty-four.

Car Insurance—Student understands that Parent prefers the Student obtain her own car insurance policy. However, Student may desire to remain covered by the family car insurance policy. Parent agrees to allow Student to remain on the family car insurance policy so long as it is permitted by the law and so long as Student remains accident free and free from moving traffic violations (tickets). Student will promptly obtain her own car insurance policy no later than thirty days following an at-fault accident or a moving traffic violation. She may enlist the advice of Parent in obtaining her own insurance. At a minimum, Student agrees to obtain coverage and keep her automobile continuously covered, as required by state law in Texas and/or her state of residence during the agreement period.

Fuel—This represents a modest fuel allowance for transportation at the school and to and from Parent's residence from time to time. Current fuel cost is about (cost) per gallon. Approximately (amount) per year will purchase 240 gallons of fuel. At twenty miles per gallon, this provides for 4,800 miles per year.

Health/co-pay—Most health insurance plans require a co-payment for general office visits and specialist visits. These typically cost \$20–\$35 per visit. In addition, prescription drugs are rarely fully covered by a health plan. Some prescriptions (such as birth control) are either not covered at all, or require special circumstances for coverage. This line item provides financial support for doctor-visit co-payments and the purchase of over-the-counter and/ or prescription medicines (including birth control). A reasonable budget for healthy young adults would be on the order of (\$cost) per month on average. This particular line item is worthy of highlighting and drawing Student's attention toward monitoring it closely. Student will need to pay any expenditure above the budgeted amount.

Books—This line item includes costs associated with textbooks, workbooks, and other material required by each class for completion of studies. Notebook paper, and related school supplies are part of this budgeted amount. Student should be advised that many books can be purchased used at large discounts, and that books can be returned for store credit following the successful completion of a course. Similarly, many books can be purchased online at discounts or "traded" between friends to reduce costs. The books tend to become more expensive as classes become more specialized toward the end of a degree program; however, the increased costs can be offset by having a larger network of friends to "trade/share" and by "learning the system" of advanced purchases (for example).

Dues—Often, college students choose to affiliate themselves with a social or academic organization. Parent encourages Student to explore various affiliates and associate with one early in her college career. The budgeted amount provides for ($cost) in dues plus an additional ($cost) per year for the purchase of T-shirts or toward other group activities.

Clothing—This conservative line item provides for the essentials only. Also for the senior year it is appropriate to consider the purchase of an "interview suit" to be used during on-campus recruiting activities or for employment visits. The budget does not provide for special-occasion attire or formal wear. Parent acknowledges Student's concern that special-occasion dresses could be part of an organization's requirements, and may provide up to ($cost) one time to subsidize that expense with no less than six weeks' notice. Student is advised to be prudent with clothing purchases during her college tenure. She will be expected to pay for her own wardrobe beyond the limited necessities afforded by this budget—similar to how an adult on her own would be expected to purchase for herself.

Phone—Student must transfer her existing mobile number into her own name as soon as possible. This amount does not cover Student's typical phone charges, although it does represent a sufficient support to provide basic phone service via landline or mobile services. Student acknowledges she uses extensive text messaging services as part of her cell phone usage. She may need to separately budget and fund her use of Internet-based and text-based services. This may be an area where Student will have difficulty maintaining her expenditures within the budgeted limit.

Personal Care—This line item provides for purchase of basic personal care items.

Miscellaneous—This line item provides for ($amount) per month of nonitemized expenditures. These expenses do not require a receipt or evidence of how the funds are used.

Clarify What Is Out of Scope

Of all the sections contained in the College Contract™, this section is at times amusing, and in other instances very powerful. When transferring accountability and responsibility to your newly minted adult, this section provides the opportunity to communicate in clear terms what the student will be responsible for. Again—authentic dialogue!

Remember, the College Contract™ is about authentic communication. Here, you list the things that you are unwilling to pay for no matter what. This does not mean you are against these things necessarily. It simply means that you will not pay for your student's decisions to pursue these.

You know your child well, and may be able to predict something not on the example list below. Some items on the list will provide you an opportunity to talk through an important issue. Other items may be less significant, but are appropriate to list nonetheless.

7. Out of Scope

List things you are unwilling to pay for no matter what.

This does not mean you are against these things, necessarily.

It simply means you will not pay for your student's decisions to pursue these.

EXAMPLE

To clarify items that may otherwise be confusing, this section outlines expenditures that are explicitly out of scope and not covered by this agreement. Student acknowledges and agrees that these items are not included in the budget. There is no intention and no obligation for Parent to underwrite, subsidize, or otherwise pay for these expenses in any way. All expenses listed here are out of scope and must be 100 percent paid by Student through sources other than Parent.

- Abortion expenses.

- Bank overdrafts and overage charges; investments.

- Beauty supplies or services such as hair coloring/styling, facials, manicures, pedicures, waxing, and massage.

- Cigarettes, liquor, illegal drugs, and paraphernalia.

- Cosmetic dentistry, such as tooth whitening; cosmetic surgery.

- Credit card origination fees or interest expenses; gambling debt.

- Damages, fines, or other fees incurred related to the operation of a vehicle by other authorized individuals on Student's behalf or with Student's permission.

- Formal or informal wear for special events, including dances, weddings, showers, and school celebrations, except where Student uses funds already being provided under this agreement.

- Fun money; entertainment expenses including movies, miniature golf, etc. not already covered within the "miscellaneous" budgeted line item.

- Furniture of any type.

- Health and fitness club memberships, except where these are covered under fees paid for tuition or other fees required by the learning institution.

- Hobby expenses such as a scrapbook, art collection, music collection.

- International studies requiring travel, unless these expenses fall within their respective budgeted line items—such as tuition.

- Laptop or desktop technology; devices including mobile phones and PDAs.

- Legal fees related to criminal or civil charges.

- Linen, including towels and sheets.

- Other damages originating from an individual other than Student toward her possessions or items under her care.

- Parking tickets, speeding tickets, or related citations.

- Pet purchases, pet supplies, pet medical bills, other pet-related expenses.

- Pots, pans, other kitchen items (note: a "care package" will be provided one time). For clarification the care package will have an approximate value of $100–$200.

- Promissory notes or other financial commitments not explicitly agreed to in this document by Parent.

- Tanning memberships; tattoos, body piercing, or removal costs for such items.

- Travel expenses other than fuel; vacation expenses.

- Weight loss programs, energy supplements, or diet pills/drinks other than if these are purchases as part of the "food" budget already accounted for.

Agree What Is Personal Property

This section will be very easy to write for some parents and their children. But there may be some instances where a shared item is assumed to be "owned" by the student, whereas the parent believes it to belong to the family at large.

To illustrate, if a large-screen television were previously purchased as a family gift to a child to be placed in a game room or common area, is this the personal property of the child, or does it belong to the family?

Because your child is now an adult, it is reasonable that he or she might want to remove and fully claim possessions.

On the flip side, a newly minted adult may not have the space or capacity to store some personal items yet. It would be reasonable for the parents to set a timetable for how much longer those items can be stored and secured for the new adult.

The concept of a "starter kit" is also common among many families. This is a way for the family to help the new adult get off to a good start—especially when moving away from home for the first time.

A starter kit will probably be assembled from some existing items around the home, but may also include some newly purchased items. Including mention of a starter kit can be a fun and collaborative way to lighten up some of the more burdensome parts of the College Contract™ process.

EXAMPLE

This section provides an inventory of personal property belonging to Student, which will remain in Student's possession. Student may take some of these items to an alternate location, such as her new residence. Some of these may remain at the family residence, during the agreement period. Student's personal property may remain at the family residence throughout the agreement period, but must be removed within one year of Student's completion of the four-year degree program or the termination of this agreement, whichever comes first. Some lesser items may not be inventoried in this list. For completeness, only items with values of $100 or more are in this list.

- Bed, mattress, bed frame and headboard

- Nightstand

- Dresser

- Mirror

- TV

- Boom box

- DVD player

- Desktop computer

- Car/Truck

Starter Kit

As would be done for most new adults moving away from home, a starter kit will be collected and provided to Student as a gift. This serves to accelerate Student's independent living away from the family residence. The starter kit will include household items, some of which are "gently used"—others of which will be purchased new, on behalf of Student. The precise inventory of these items has not been decided upon as of the drafting of this agreement. However, the following list provides a general idea of what might be in the starter kit:

- Small electric appliances (e.g., toaster)

- Cleaning supplies

- Pots/pans/dishes

- Bed linen and towels

- Hand tools

- Household repair items

- Small furnishings for dorm (e.g., lamps, small table)

"I told him to move out! I just forgot to say by when." Unknown.

The United States has a lot of "boomerang children"—or adult children who move back into the family residence. College-bound adults sometimes attend a school close to the family residence, continuing to live at home. Sometimes a student lives away from the family during fall and spring semesters, but returns during summer break. This section outlines variations related to Student's choice related to the family home during the agreement period.

9. Family Residence

Case 1 – live at home

Case 2 – on weekends

Case 3 – over summer

Case 4 - others

EXAMPLE

Student agrees she needs to be fully moved out of the family home within six months of finishing school. If she quits school, she needs to be fully moved out within six months after quitting.

Student may, at her sole discretion, keep and store her personal possessions at the family residence within the bedroom designated as her room. This is true only during the effective period of this agreement plus six months as described in the earlier paragraph. In no instance will an illegal item or substance be stored in the family home. Student commits to refrain from possessing or allowing possession of an illegal substance within the family home or property. If any such substance exists at any time, to Student's knowledge, she will immediately destroy it.

Case 1

If Student chooses to continue living at the family residence while attending University of University, Junior College, or a similarly close institution, this section identifies the expectations, rules, and agreements.

Rent: Per-month rent will be assessed at $125/month for each full or partial month. Student will sign an invoice acknowledging the amount will be subtracted from the rent budget.

Food: Because of the difficulty in separating food purchases in this instance, the per-month food allowance/budget during this period will be dropped from $120/month to $40/month in cash and Student will sign an invoice acknowledging the full $120/month in food allowance ($40 cash plus $80 as her "share" of food from the family pantry). In this instance, Student may make special requests for grocery items, but should not expect, and certainly should not demand, that the items be purchased on her behalf. It will be incumbent upon Student to supply herself with any special-needs food items not already provided in the family pantry (through the reduced $40 allowance, or other means).

Access: During this period, Student will have free access to the family residence through the use of a house key. Access to friends and others will be permitted except for restrictions through house curfews and appropriateness. In all instances, Student's guests will be expected to leave the house prior to 1:00 a.m. In no instance will overnight stays be permitted for men, except that, in limited situations with explicit prior approval, a male guest may be permitted to spend the night sleeping on a separate floor. Parent acknowledges that Student will be an adult during this agreement period and may at her discretion choose to not live at the family residence and that she may have different standards regarding mixed-gender sleeping arrangements. In turn, Student acknowledges that Parent may establish house rules for the family residence, and that this specific ideal remains intact regardless. Should Student become married during the agreement period, this option (of living at the family residence) would expire within one month of the wedding date.

Rules: Parent retains all rights to establish and maintain family residence rules. Student agrees to comply with those rules that may, at Parent's sole discretion, be modified with two days' notice to Student.

Participation: Student may be invited to participate in family activities, but will not be required to participate.

Case 2

If Student chooses to return to living at the family residence during the summer session—and potentially attend University of University, Junior College, or perhaps work during this time—this section identifies the expectations, rules, and agreements.

Rent: Per-month rent will be assessed at $120/month for June, July, and August. Student will sign an invoice acknowledging the amount will be subtracted from the rent budget.

Food: Because of the difficulty in separating food purchases in this instance, the per-month food allowance/budget during this period will be dropped from $120/month to $40/month in cash and Student will sign an invoice acknowledging the full $120/month in food allowance ($40 cash plus $80 as her "share" of food from the family pantry). In this instance, Student may make special requests for grocery items, but should not expect, and certainly should not demand, that the items be purchased on her behalf. It will be incumbent upon Student to supply herself with any special-needs food items not already provided in the family pantry (through the reduced $40 allowance, or other means).

Access: During this period, Student will have free access to the family residence through the use of a house key. Access to friends and others will be permitted except for restrictions through house curfews and appropriateness. In all instances, Student's guests will be expected to leave the house prior to 1:00 a.m. In no instance will overnight stays be permitted for men, except that, in limited situations with explicit prior approval, a male guest may be permitted to spend the night sleeping on a separate floor. Parent acknowledges that Student will be an adult during this agreement period and may at her discretion choose to not live at the family residence and that she may have different standards regarding mixed-gender sleeping arrangements. In turn, Student acknowledges that Parent may establish house rules for the family residence, and that this specific ideal remains intact regardless. Should Student become married during the agreement period, this option (of living at the family residence) would expire within one month of the wedding date.

Rules: Parent retains all rights and privileges to establish and maintain family residence rules. Student agrees to comply with those rules that may, at Parent's sole discretion, be modified with two days' notice to Student.

Participation: Student may be invited to participate in family activities, but will not be required to participate.

Case 3

If Student chooses not live at the family residence at all during the agreement period, but intends to visit on weekends from time to time, this section identifies the expectations, rules, and agreements.

Rent: No rent will be assessed against the family residence. Only the rent incurred from Student's place of residence will be counted as rent.

Food: Because Student will be visiting the family home "as a guest," the budgeted food line item will continue to remain in effect during the agreement period. No charges for food will be incurred from these infrequent visits.

Access: During this period, Student will always lock the door prior to leaving. In all instances, to the degree she is able, she should inform Parent prior to her arrival, as would any courteous guest. Access to friends and others will be permitted except for restrictions through house curfews and appropriateness. In all instances, Student's guests will be expected to leave the house prior to 1:00 a.m. In no instance will overnight stays be permitted for men, except that, in limited situations with explicit prior approval, a male guest may be permitted to spend the night sleeping on a separate floor. Parent acknowledges that Student will be an adult during this agreement period and may at her discretion choose to not stay at the family residence and that she may have different standards regarding mixed-gender sleeping arrangements. In turn, Student acknowledges that Parent may establish house rules for the family residence, and that this specific ideal remains intact regardless. Should Student become married during the agreement period, the mixed-gender sleeping restriction becomes null and void between Student and her spouse within the family home.

Rules: Parent retains all rights and privileges to establish and maintain family residence rules. Student agrees to comply with those rules that may, at Parent's sole discretion, be modified with two days' notice to Student.

Participation: Student may be invited to participate in family activities, but will not be required to participate.

Establish a Financial Table

"Without music to decorate it, time is just a bunch of boring production deadlines or dates by which bills must be paid." Frank Zappa

Sorry, Frank. This section has no musical decoration. But it does serve as the centerpiece to the entire document. Without the Financial Table, the document is not really a College Contract™.

This section requires real research by both the parent and the child. The Financial Table should document how much financial support the parent will provide to the child for each major category of spending over the course of time.

Some categories, such as health care insurance may need to be estimated because the child's insurance cost is part of the family health insurance cost. Even so, it is appropriate to explicitly list this value as a benefit to the newly minted adult.

Even if the Student lives at home, a value for the room and board should be estimated and listed on the Financial Table. This highlights the value to the Student. When the contract assumes the Student will live at home during the four years, list the estimated value on the Financial Table, but include a paragraph stating that "if the Student moves away from home, the budgeted amount for this line item will drop to zero dollars." Using this approach emphasizes the value to the student. Additionally, establish a monthly "rent" for the room to be deducted from the budget, even if no actual money changes hands.

EXAMPLE

Financial Table	Year 1	Year 2	Year 3	Year 4
Tuition	$amount	$amount	$amount	$amount
Books	$amount	$amount	$amount	$amount
Room	$amount	$amount	$amount	$amount
Food	$amount	$amount	$amount	$amount
Healthcare	$amount	$amount	$amount	$amount
Car	$amount	$amount	$amount	$amount
Car Repair	$amount	$amount	$amount	$amount
Fuel	$amount	$amount	$amount	$amount
Clothing	$amount	$amount	$amount	$amount
Phone	$amount	$amount	$amount	$amount
Dues	$amount	$amount	$amount	$amount
Personal Care	$amount	$amount	$amount	$amount
Loans	$amount	$amount	$amount	$amount

Each cell on the Financial Table represents the maximum to be paid by Parent on Student's behalf for each year, for each category of expense. Any expense incurred greater than the budgeted amount listed in each cell will not be paid, reimbursed, or otherwise satisfied by Parent. Student will be responsible for all expenses exceeding any value in the cells of the Financial Table.

Expenses less than the budgeted amount will be accumulated as an "underage." At the completion of Student's four-year degree program, Parent may present to Student up to 50 percent of the accumulated savings (underage) as a cash payment. This is solely at the Parent's discretion.

For example, if the total tuition cost equals $14,800 rather than the budgeted $24,800 due to low tuition rates and/or scholarships received, then Student may receive $5,000 of the $10,000 savings at the completion of the degree.

The health insurance line item represents an approximate value of Student's portion of the family health insurance plan currently in place. If she marries or takes out her own health policy the health insurance provided will drop to $0.

Identify Special Circumstances

This section aims to anticipate events that might significantly alter the terms of the agreement, should they occur. Most of the items listed in this section might be described as low-probability but high-impact events.

This section serves to answer the "what-if" scenarios that might concern you or might concern your child. This is kind of a sad section—but important. The authentic dialogue here pre-empts difficult discussions at a later time.

EXAMPLE

Marriage. In the event of marriage, Student's participation in the family health insurance plan will not be permitted by the carrier. In this event, Student will necessarily be required to obtain her own health insurance policy, which will not be underwritten, paid, or partially paid by Parent.

Pregnancy. In the event of Student's pregnancy during the agreement period, no changes in the timing of or amounts of support should be assumed. Parent, at his sole discretion, may allow for a six-month gap, and subsequent six-month extension to the timetable and support table.

War. In the event of war requiring the enlistment of Student in the armed services, all the terms of the Agreement remain in effect (but with a suspended time frame). Once the student returns from any required enlistment, the Agreement restarts from the most recent previous period (college semester).

Illness/Injury. In the event of a severe illness and/or injury, requiring hospitalization of Student, Parent may, at his sole discretion, allow for a six-month gap, and subsequent six-month extension to the timetable and support table.

Job Loss. In the event of a job loss, job change, or a similar job-related circumstance that substantially alters Parent's income, Parent will make a genuine effort to continue support as described in the Financial Table, but reserves the right to cancel the remaining agreement indefinitely in this specific case of substantial change in income through job-related events.

Death. In the event of Parent's death, a sufficient level of life insurance coverage will be maintained by Parent to continue the agreement as outlined, except that, a six-month gap and subsequent six-month extension may be necessary beginning on the date of Parent's death to allow his wife sufficient time to collect on insurance policies. Parent's wife will continue with the remaining agreement, except for the possibility of a six-month gap and extension, which would be at her sole discretion.

School Change. In the event of Student choosing to change schools, this agreement remains intact and will not be extended or otherwise revised upward (increased financial support). This is important to understand and note in that sometimes course work does not fully transfer from one school to another, and a variety of other start-up costs may be required to enable such a transfer. This agreement explicitly excludes any and all such costs associated with changing schools. Should she decide to change schools, student will be fully and 100 percent responsible for any and all increased costs above those listed in the Financial Table associated with school changes.

Drop Out. In the event Student drops out of school for a period of time for reasons other than severe health issues requiring hospitalization, severe injury requiring hospitalization, acts of war requiring Student's participation with the US armed services, or other acts of God, this agreement becomes null and void, whereas no additional financial support is required from Parent to Student, and Student will not at some later time request or demand that it be provided.

Include Signatures

This section outlines the "legalese" part of the document. Even though the College Contract™ is intended to help you and your child make a budget and improve your communication with each other, realistically, it also serves as a potentially legally binding document. But beyond that, your child deserves to be introduced to the concepts of a contract and the differences between verbal agreements and written agreements.

I recommend you consider including six components in the final Signature Section of your College Contract™.

- Further Assurances

- Construction and Interpretation

- Entire Agreement

- Invalid Provisions

- Advice of Counsel

- Notarization

Each of these is described below.

Further Assurances

When entering into an agreement where additional paperwork or filings might be required after the agreement is signed, you may want to add a "further assurances" clause, similar to the one below:

In connection with this Agreement, each party to this Agreement will execute and deliver any additional documents and instruments and perform any additional acts that may be necessary or appropriate to perform their obligations under this Agreement and the transactions contemplated hereby.

Construction and Interpretation

While the College Contract™ process is not intended to be punitive or used in a heavy-handed way, there is a possibility that you and your child may need to have a particular issue resolved by a court. I hope not. But just in case, you should be aware that courts have, over time, established general rules of legal construction or interpretation when reviewing legal documents.

If there is ambiguity in a document, the ambiguity will be construed against the person who drafted the document (in this case—you). Because of this, add a "legal construction" or "interpretation" clause to your legal agreement. This reduces the number of uncertainties that may arise in interpreting the document. An example of a legal construction clause is below:

This Agreement will in all events be construed as a whole, according to its fair meaning, and not strictly for or against a party merely because that party drafted the Agreement. The headings, titles, and captions contained in this Agreement are merely for reference and do not define, limit, extend, or describe the scope of this Agreement or any provision herein. Unless the context requires otherwise, (a) the gender (or lack of gender) of all words used in this Agreement includes the masculine, feminine, and neuter, and (b) the word "including" means "including, without limitation."

Entire Agreement

A written legal agreement is usually the final, complete statement of agreement between two parties on a particular subject. Add an "entire agreement" clause to clarify that previous communications or correspondence should not change the terms of the final written agreement. Here is an example:

This Agreement constitutes the entire agreement of the parties relating to the subject matter addressed in this Agreement. This Agreement supersedes all prior agreements, communications, or contracts between the parties with respect to the subject matter addressed in this Agreement, whether oral or written.

Invalid Provisions

This book is not intended to provide you with the various nuances of the law, or for that matter to teach how to write a legally binding contract. In all instances, you should enlist the services of a licensed attorney for those opinions and advice.

If you have a concern that any term within an agreement may be illegal or unenforceable under any applicable law (federal, state, or local), you should consult a licensed attorney for advice. Your attorney may be able to clarify the matter for you. If there is still a question about whether a particular provision may exceed the limitations of applicable law, a common approach is to include a "severance" or "invalid provisions" clause in your agreement. Here is an example:

If any provision of this Agreement is held to be invalid, illegal, or unenforceable under any present or future law, then that provision will be fully severable. This Agreement will be construed and enforced as if the invalid, illegal, or unenforceable provision had never comprised a part of this Agreement, and the remaining provisions of this Agreement will remain in full force. Remaining portions of the Agreement will not be affected by the illegal, invalid, or unenforceable provision or by its severance from this Agreement.

Advice of Counsel

A defense often raised to enforce an agreement is that a party did not understand the terms of the agreement or did not have the advice of an attorney before the agreement was signed. (In this instance, most College Contract™ Agreements will be written without the assistance of legal counsel.) A good clause to add to any legal agreement is a statement that each party understands the agreement and has either enlisted legal counsel, or has had the opportunity to seek legal counsel. An example of such a clause is shown below.

Each party to this Agreement represents and warrants to each other party that such party has read and fully understands the terms and provisions hereof, has had an opportunity to review this Agreement with legal counsel (or has otherwise chosen to review the Agreement without legal counsel), and has executed this Agreement based upon such party's own judgment and advice of independent legal counsel (if sought).

Notarization

A College Contract™ does not have to be notarized. But, I recommend you do notarize the document for two reasons. First, the very act of signing a document for notarization underscores the importance of the document. But also, the document should serve as a binding Agreement between you and your adult child. In the case of divorced parents, there may be an agreement in place between the divorced parents requiring one or both of the parents to provide certain financial support to their children for higher education.

Requirements for notarization vary from state to state. Consult a licensed attorney to make certain your documents meet applicable requirements. Notarization is usually required when dealing with wills, real property documents, or documents filed in the public records. In the case of divorced parents, the College Contract™ may be appropriate to file along with previously filed court documents associated with the terms of the divorce. You may also choose to have a document notarized if there is any concern that the person signing the document will later deny his or her signature on the documents.

The appropriate form of notarization varies from state to state, as noted above (again, check with a lawyer to make sure your form is correct). Below you is an example notarization method.

Sample notarization for an individual:

Notarization

STATE OF _____ §
COUNTY OF _____ §

Before me, the undersigned authority, on this day personally appeared {your name and your child's name}, known to me to be the persons whose names are subscribed to the foregoing instrument, and upon their oath acknowledged to me that they have executed the same for the purposes and consideration therein expressed.

GIVEN UNDER MY HAND AND SEAL OF OFFICE THIS _____ DAY OF _____, 20___.

_____
NOTARY PUBLIC IN AND FOR {county} COUNTY, {state}

What Is an Adult?

In the US, our collective definition of an "adult" differs from beliefs of a hundred years ago. Even within the past two generations, what we collectively view as an "adult" is different from what many of us used to think. One way of illustrating this point is by noting the prolific use of the word "guy" rather than "man" for males under the age of thirty years old—as in "He is a good guy."

To some degree, this is understandable—life expectancy has increased. Perhaps the path to adulthood should take longer. On the other hand, recent decades have perhaps unintentionally encouraged legal adults to remain adolescent in many ways—remaining financially dependent on their parents even after receiving a four-year college degree. I'd like to contribute to reversing that trend.

My hope is that ten years from now we more frequently hear "He is a good man" for the twenty-three-year-old college graduate receiving a job promotion. For the adult children choosing to live with their parents, I hope it is out of mutual closeness and family belongingness. I hope we rarely see this due to financial necessity or emotional dependency. I hope we collectively reduce the number of "adult teenagers." Let's increase the number of adults who happen to be in their twenties.

Authenticity with your emerging adult is part of the answer. This chapter is adapted from a paper titled "The role of acculturation in the emerging adulthood of aboriginal college students" by Charissa S.L. Cheah and Larry J. Nelson, published in the International Journal of Behavioral

Development, 2004. Below, find a list of attributes used in the study. These items are sometimes used as a measure as to whether someone is an adult or not.

A good exercise for you and your emerging adult child would be to review and discuss these lists. Identify which of these attributes most significantly define an "adult" in your eyes. Not all of these will apply to your definition of an adult. This list may miss a few. But, after scanning through the list, have a discussion with your child—so he or she clearly understands your point of view. Listen to your child's viewpoint with open ears.

The College Contract™ quickens the path to adulthood. The process accelerates independence, norm compliance, and role transitions. Other books and resources focus on interdependence and family capacity.

How do you define an "Adult"?

Independence
Norm compliance
Individual role transitions
Interdependence
Family capacities

Independence

Accept responsibility for the consequences of one's own actions

Decide on personal beliefs and values independently of parents or other influences

Establish equal relationship with parents

Financially independent of parents

No longer living in parents' household

Not deeply tied to parents emotionally

Norm compliance

Avoid becoming drunk

Avoid committing petty crimes like vandalism and shoplifting

Avoid drunk driving

Avoid illegal drugs

Avoid use of profanity/vulgar language

Drive safely and close to the speed limit

Have no more than one sexual partner

Use contraception if sexually active and not trying to conceive a child

Individual Role transitions

Become employed full-time

Finish education

Settle into a long-term career

Interdependence

Become less self-oriented, develop greater consideration for others

Commit to long-term love relationships

Learn always to have good control over your emotions

Make lifelong commitments to others

Family capacities

Become capable of caring for children

Become capable of keeping family physically safe

Become capable of running a household

Become capable of supporting a family financially

Get married

Have at least one child

Purchase a house

Who Are the Millenials?

"Among democratic nations each generation is a new people." Alexis de Tocqueville

The press has given "Generation Y" several interesting names/labels. Among these titles are: Baby Busters, Boomlets, Digital Generation, Echo Boomers, Gaming Generation, Generation Next, Generation WHY, I Generation, Millenniums, Net Generation, Netizens, and Nexers.

We are different from our children. One obvious way is that our children have never experienced life without computers—everything is "one click away" to them. We were different from our parents—so these differences shouldn't come as any huge surprise. Some would argue that our children are the most "hovered over" generation ever in our country. Certainly, as a group, they have had significant parental advocacy.

Sure, we also have a lot of things in common with our children. But perhaps it is appropriate to take pause for a moment and reflect on the differences just a bit.

As a quick heads-up, your child is probably more comfortable with speed and change than you are. Your child probably gets impatient with any perceived lack of progress. Likely, your child values guidance, but also expects to be given respect (even if it has not yet been "earned"). Your child probably wants to "make a difference"—and would especially be drawn to it given the opportunity to work with friends and on teams.

This chapter attempts only to highlight that some differences exist—and that we should expect our dialogue with our emerging adult child to have some hiccups. This is especially true in the drafting and subsequent management of a College Contract™. Done well, your child will benefit from improved financial discipline and from the wisdom of your past mistakes and successes. Done well, you too will benefit from less uncertainty and improved dialogue with your child.

It would be both unfair and inaccurate to categorize any one age group as each having the same collective values and attributes of all other individuals in that age group. Still, there are some general themes that warrant discussion and consideration. Below are some generalized themes associated with three generations. Consider using these lists as an additional way for you and your emerging adult to learn about each other and improve your College Contract™ experience.

Baby Boomers (Seek Success) born 1948–1962

Baby Boomer

Avoids hostile environments, if possible
Enjoys learning
Needs respect from others
Usually success driven
Wants financial prosperity
Wants to do something "worthwhile"
Wants to use skills and talents
Willing to "go an extra mile"

Composite list from multiple publicly available sources

Generation X (Seek Balance) born 1963–1980

Generation-X

Needs to feel a part of important decisions

Readily takes calculated risk

Seeks work-life balance

Skeptical of others until proven otherwise

Tends to be self-reliant

Work is about the outcome, not the hours

Composite list from multiple publicly available sources

Generation Y (Seek Connection) born 1981–1993

Generation-Y

Assumes everything is mobile/instant

Characterized by realism and street savvy

Likes group action over individual action

Needs non-monetary rewards

Often tenacious, obstinate, and resolute

Tends to be optimistic

Wants to "belong" to something

Composite list from multiple publicly available sources

Whether or not these lists accurately depict you and your child, it is worthwhile to explore the similarities and differences between you and your child. Now that your child is a legal adult, you are in a great position to help him or her become a full and independent adult. Notice too, the importance of authentic dialogue to your child's generation.

This book aims to help you and your college-bound adult child craft a College Contract™ fitting your unique situation. Hopefully, this book will help avert many of the situations outlined in the chapter called "Reality check." The process reasonably takes three months to complete—not because the contract itself takes that long to write—but rather because you will think of things and discover ideas during the three-month period together.

Access downloadable College Contract™ templates as other resources at:

www.CollegeContract.com

My Love Note

"To a father growing old nothing is dearer than a daughter."
Euripides BC 480-406.

To Danielle, my daughter:

Our contract sometimes seemed overwhelming, unnecessary, and even offensive. But, I think you now recognize it was made out of love. Our relationship changed on your eighteenth birthday. The change has not diminished my love for you. I will always pray for your well-being and great things for you. I think because of the contract you and I have had less disagreement. You now better understand how responsibility and accountability go together. I hope, through this, I've been a better teacher for you and few things have been unreasonable. I am proud of you and I'm certain God has good things in store for you. By the way, I haven't the foggiest of who Euripides was, but I think I agree with him. Love, your dad.

Made in the USA
San Bernardino, CA
05 April 2015